THE LOVE YOU'VE BEEN WAITING FOR

SECRETS TO FINDING AND CHOOSING THE RIGHT PARTNER

DAVID R. ADDISON

DEDICATION

To those who dare to seek love amidst the chaos of modern relationships, may your journey be filled with self-discovery, courage, and the joy of finding the partner who resonates with your heart. This book is dedicated to all the souls who believe in the transformative power of love and are committed to nurturing the connections that enrich our lives.

ACKNOWLEDGEMENT

I extend my heartfelt gratitude to the many individuals who have inspired this book through their stories, insights, and unwavering belief in the beauty of love. To my friends and family, thank you for your constant encouragement and for sharing your own experiences, which have enriched my understanding of relationships. Your honesty and openness have been a guiding light as I explored the complexities of love, and I am grateful for the lessons learned along the way.

I also wish to acknowledge the countless authors, psychologists, and relationship experts whose work laid the foundation for my exploration of love and partnerships. Their research and insights provided a wealth of knowledge that shaped this book, and I am thankful for their dedication to helping others navigate the often-tumultuous waters of relationships. To everyone who has contributed to the conversation about love, your voices have been instrumental in creating a deeper understanding of what it means to find and choose the right partner.

TABLE OF CONTENT

INTRODUCTION

Love is one of the most fundamental emotions humans' experiences, driving countless decisions and shaping lives. At its core, the search for love is about finding that one person with whom you can share your life, someone who truly understands, respects, and complements you. In today's world, this journey has evolved, becoming more complex but also more rewarding for those willing to put in the work. Understanding love and relationships begins with recognizing the vital role they play in personal happiness and overall well-being.

A compatible life partner is more than just someone to share everyday moments with. The right person can offer emotional support in times of need, encourage you to pursue your dreams, and share in life's most memorable experiences. Studies have shown that individuals who are in healthy, fulfilling relationships tend to live longer, are happier, and experience less stress. There is a profound connection between emotional satisfaction and physical health. When two people are aligned in values, goals, and aspirations, their relationship acts as a foundation upon which a lifetime of joy and stability is built. On the other hand, when individuals settle for a relationship that lacks compatibility, the discord can seep into other areas of life—impacting mental health, career satisfaction, and even physical well-being.

The importance of finding the right partner cannot be overstated. Relationships are not just about companionship but about fostering growth and creating an environment in which both people can thrive. Compatibility ensures that both partners share a common vision for their future, helping to avoid misunderstandings and conflicts. While passion and excitement may be the initial spark, it's the deeper connection that stands the test of time, nurturing the relationship through its highs and lows. Love, at its best, brings out the finest qualities in each person and creates a bond that transcends superficial attractions.

However, the path to finding this ideal partner is often far from straightforward, especially in the modern dating landscape. Dating has transformed dramatically in recent years, influenced by technology, societal changes, and evolving expectations. With the rise of online dating platforms, social media, and dating apps, meeting potential partners has never been easier, yet paradoxically, it has also never been more challenging. In an age where everything is available at the swipe of a finger, the sheer volume of options can be overwhelming, making it difficult to focus on meaningful connections. The ease of access to multiple people at once can sometimes create a culture of disposability, where people are viewed more like commodities than potential life partners.

Social media plays a significant role in shaping modern relationships. People are often more focused on crafting the perfect image online, presenting a version of themselves that may not align with who they truly are. The pressure to curate a flawless online persona can sometimes lead to superficial connections, where appearances are prioritized over substance. Furthermore, the fast-paced nature of communication today—where instant messaging and constant notifications are the norm—can lead to misunderstandings, miscommunications, and rushed decisions when it comes to love. Relationships that once took time to develop are now often expected to blossom at lightning speed, creating unrealistic expectations and leaving little room for genuine growth.

With so many factors complicating the search for love, patience and preparation have become more crucial than ever. The journey to finding a lasting relationship is not one that should be rushed, nor is it one that should be entered into without introspection and readiness. Before seeking out a partner, it is essential to take a step back and evaluate oneself. Self-awareness is key to understanding what you truly need in a relationship, rather than what societal pressures or fleeting desires may dictate. Knowing your strengths, weaknesses, values, and long-term goals will help you identify a partner who complements you, rather than simply someone who fills a temporary void.

Preparation also involves healing from past relationships and experiences. Entering a new relationship without addressing emotional baggage from the past can create unnecessary friction and set unrealistic expectations. It's important to process any hurt, disappointment, or trauma from previous relationships so that you can approach new connections with a clear mind and an open heart. Emotional wounds, when left unattended, can manifest as trust issues, insecurities, or the tendency to sabotage new relationships before they have the chance to develop.

Patience is the final ingredient that ties everything together. The process of finding the right partner should not be seen as a race, but rather as a journey that requires time and reflection. Rushing into a relationship because of societal expectations or the fear of being alone can lead to settling for less than what you deserve. True compatibility takes time to uncover, and it is only by allowing a relationship to develop at its own pace that you can truly gauge whether it has the potential to last. Waiting for the right person, rather than jumping into relationships impulsively, increases the likelihood of finding someone who shares your values and long-term vision for the future.

Ultimately, love is not just about finding someone who makes you happy in the short term, but about building a relationship that will stand the test of time. The right partner will enhance your life, helping you to grow and become the best version of yourself. In turn, you will do the same for them, creating a partnership that is not only rooted in love but also in mutual respect and understanding. Navigating the complexities of the modern dating world may be challenging, but with self-awareness, preparation, and patience, the reward of a fulfilling and lasting relationship is well worth the effort.

As you embark on this journey, remember that finding love is about much more than simply crossing paths with someone who sparks your interest. It is about being intentional in your pursuit, taking the time to truly know yourself and what you need in a partner, and being willing to put in the work to build a relationship that is both meaningful and sustainable. The love you've been waiting for is not something that can be rushed or forced, but something that grows organically when the right conditions are in place—when you are ready to receive it, and when the person standing beside you is equally prepared for the journey ahead.

CHAPTER 1: THE FOUNDATION OF SELF-LOVE

Finding a loving, compatible partner begins with understanding the most important person in your life—you. The journey to true love starts with self-awareness, healing, and confidence. These elements form the foundation of a healthy, lasting relationship, allowing you to approach love with a clear understanding of what you need and deserve.

Discovering who you are is the first step in this journey. It is impossible to find someone who complements you without first understanding your own values, goals, and emotional needs. Many people rush into relationships, seeking validation or companionship, but they often overlook the critical step of self-reflection. Taking the time to explore your personal values, passions, and life goals helps you identify what truly matters to you. These are the non-negotiable aspects of your life that shape how you view the world, interact with others, and plan your future. When these core values are not aligned with a partner's, conflict is inevitable.

Begin by asking yourself the essential questions: What do you stand for? What are your priorities in life? What kind of future do you envision? Identifying these values allows you to set boundaries and standards in relationships, ensuring you do not settle for someone who doesn't share your outlook on life. Your emotional needs also play a significant role in self-awareness. Are you someone who craves affection, or do you value independence? Understanding what makes you feel loved and fulfilled emotionally helps in finding a partner who can meet those needs.

Beyond self-awareness, healing from past wounds is crucial before embarking on a new relationship. Many individuals carry emotional baggage from previous relationships— whether it's the pain of betrayal, the sting of rejection, or unresolved feelings from a breakup. These past experiences, when left unaddressed, can cloud your judgment and influence how you approach future relationships. You may find yourself projecting past hurts onto a new partner or entering relationships with a guarded heart, unable to fully trust or invest in someone new.

Healing is a process, and it often involves confronting painful memories or feelings that you've pushed aside. Give yourself permission to grieve the end of previous relationships, acknowledge the hurt, and then let go. This might involve journaling, seeking therapy, or engaging in self-care practices that allow you to process these emotions fully. Once you have healed, you can approach new relationships with a clear heart, free from the shadows of the past. This also ensures that you do not bring unresolved issues into your next relationship, which can prevent it from thriving.

Building self-confidence is the next important step on the path to love. Confidence is attractive because it shows that you know your worth and are comfortable in your skin. It also allows you to set healthy boundaries and communicate effectively with potential partners. Confidence does not mean arrogance; rather, it's about having a deep sense of self-worth that isn't dependent on external validation. When you enter a relationship from a place of confidence, you are less likely to compromise your values or settle for less than you deserve.

There are practical ways to build self-confidence, and they all start with self-care. Taking care of your physical, emotional, and mental health boosts your self-esteem and reinforces the belief that you are worthy of love and respect. Engage in activities that make you feel good about yourself, whether that's exercising, learning new skills, or pursuing hobbies you're passionate about. Surround yourself with supportive, positive people who uplift and encourage you.

When you focus on nurturing yourself, you become more confident in your ability to attract a partner who values and respects you for who you are.

Confidence also comes from learning to love yourself unconditionally. This means accepting your flaws and imperfections while recognizing your strengths. No one is perfect, and holding yourself to unrealistic standards can damage your self-esteem. Embrace the unique qualities that make you who you are, and remember that the right partner will love you not despite your flaws but because of them.

Finally, creating a vision of the right relationship is essential to manifesting the love you desire. Many people have a vague idea of what they want in a partner but haven't taken the time to clearly define their ideal relationship. Without a clear vision, it's easy to get swept up in infatuation or settle for a relationship that doesn't meet your long-term needs. Take the time to create a mental picture of the type of relationship you want. This isn't about creating a checklist of superficial qualities, such as height or profession, but rather focusing on the deeper aspects of a relationship.

What kind of emotional connection do you want to share with your partner? How do you envision your life together in terms of values, goals, and shared experiences? Picture how your partner supports and complements you, how you handle conflicts, and how you grow together. Visualizing the right relationship helps you recognize it when it appears, and it also helps you avoid distractions or settling for relationships that do not align with your vision.

It's important to remember that this vision should remain flexible. While it's essential to have a clear idea of what you want, it's equally important to be open to the unexpected. Sometimes, love doesn't show up in the exact package you expected, but it can still meet your needs in ways you didn't anticipate. Stay open to possibilities, but always remain true to your core values and emotional needs.

By focusing on self-awareness, healing, confidence, and vision, you lay the groundwork for a strong, fulfilling relationship. Before seeking love from someone else, ensure that you are in the best possible place emotionally and mentally. A relationship that is built on mutual respect, shared values, and emotional compatibility is far more likely to stand the test of time. The foundation of self-love is what will allow you to attract the partner you've been waiting for and create a relationship that is both joyful and lasting.

CHAPTER 2: WHAT ARE YOU LOOKING FOR IN A PARTNER?

Understanding what you truly need in a partner is an essential step in forming a lasting relationship. Too often, people confuse superficial desires with fundamental necessities, leading to disappointment when the relationship doesn't stand the test of time. The key to finding the right partner is distinguishing between your needs and wants and ensuring that your core values, life goals, and personality traits are compatible with theirs. Moreover, identifying deal breakers is crucial to avoiding future heartache and wasted time on relationships that cannot flourish.

The first step is understanding the difference between your needs and wants in a relationship. Needs are the essential qualities that a partner must have for a relationship to be successful. These are the traits or values that directly influence your happiness, emotional well-being, and future together. For example, if you value honesty, trust is a need. If you want to build a family, the desire for children becomes a non-negotiable need. Needs reflect deeper aspects of life that determine compatibility on a fundamental level.

Wants, on the other hand, are often superficial and based on fleeting desires or preferences. While they may enhance attraction, they do not necessarily contribute to the long-term success of a relationship. A partner's physical appearance, financial status, or specific hobbies might initially catch your attention, but these traits often change or become less important as the relationship progresses. It's easy to become distracted by the excitement of fulfilling a want, but without the foundation of meeting your needs, the relationship may struggle in the long term.

Recognizing the difference between needs and wants allows you to prioritize the qualities that truly matter. Ask yourself what is non-negotiable for you. For example, do you need a partner who communicates openly and effectively? Someone who shares your vision of the future? Once you've identified your needs, you can more easily filter out potential partners who do not align with your essential values, saving yourself time and emotional investment in relationships that are unlikely to succeed.

Next, understanding your core values and life goals is critical in finding the right partner. Values shape the way we live our lives, interact with others, and make decisions. If two people's core values are misaligned, their relationship will face constant friction. Core values include things like your beliefs about family, career, religion, and overall life philosophy. For instance, if you value family above all else but your partner prioritizes career ambitions to the exclusion of family time, this mismatch can create tension and dissatisfaction over time.

When evaluating a potential partner, it's important to have honest conversations about these values early on. Discuss your expectations around major life decisions like marriage, children, financial management, and where you envision living in the future. These are fundamental topics that can dramatically influence your relationship's success. When your values and goals align, you create a solid foundation for mutual respect and understanding, which is key to navigating the inevitable challenges that arise in any long-term relationship.

Personality traits also play a crucial role in relationship dynamics, and compatibility goes beyond surface-level attraction. While it's tempting to focus on physical chemistry or shared interests, the deeper connection stems from understanding how your personalities complement one another. Some people may be naturally more introverted or extroverted, while others have different approaches to handling conflict or expressing emotions.

One useful framework for understanding personality compatibility is the concept of attachment styles. Psychologists categorize attachment styles into four types: secure, anxious, avoidant, and fearful-avoidant. These styles are based on how individuals relate to others, particularly in romantic relationships. Understanding your attachment style—and that of your partner—can give you insights into how you both approach intimacy, conflict, and communication. For instance, a secure attachment style often leads to healthy, balanced relationships, while an anxious or avoidant style may result in challenges related to trust and closeness.

Another factor to consider is how well your partner's personality complements yours. Do you balance each other out in areas like decision-making, problem-solving, and emotional expression? Or do your differences create unnecessary conflict? While it's normal for partners to have different personalities, compatibility is about finding harmony in these differences and learning to appreciate them rather than allowing them to become sources of friction. For example, one partner might be more organized and practical, while the other is spontaneous and creative. This difference can either be a source of strength or conflict, depending on how well you both adapt to and respect each other's traits.

In addition to personality traits, deal breakers are an essential aspect of evaluating potential partners. These are the non-negotiable factors that, if present, would make a relationship untenable. Deal breakers can range from lifestyle differences to moral or ethical boundaries. For example, some people may have deal breakers related to substance abuse, infidelity, or financial irresponsibility. Others may have more specific concerns, such as a partner's unwillingness to relocate or differing views on marriage and children.

Identifying your deal breakers early on helps you avoid entering relationships that are doomed to fail. It also gives you the confidence to walk away from situations that don't serve your long-term happiness, even if you feel a strong emotional connection to the person. Many people make the mistake of overlooking deal breakers in the early stages of dating, only to face heartbreak later when these issues become insurmountable. By being clear about your boundaries from the outset, you can save yourself time and emotional energy, ensuring that you invest in relationships with real potential.

It's important to approach these conversations about needs, values, personality traits, and deal breakers with openness and honesty. Communication is the cornerstone of any successful relationship, and being upfront about what you're looking for in a partner allows both you and your potential partner to assess whether you are truly compatible. When both individuals have a clear understanding of each other's needs and values, they are better equipped to build a relationship based on mutual respect, trust, and shared goals.

In summary, understanding what you are looking for in a partner goes beyond surface-level attraction. It requires a deep awareness of your own needs, values, and deal breakers, as well as a thoughtful examination of how your personality and life goals align with those of a potential partner. By taking the time to reflect on these aspects, you increase your chances of finding a partner who complements you and contributes to a healthy, fulfilling relationship. Relationships built on shared values, compatible personalities, and mutual respect are far more likely to stand the test of time, creating a lasting partnership that enriches both your lives.

CHAPTER 3: NAVIGATING THE MODERN DATING WORLD

The modern dating landscape has transformed dramatically with the rise of technology, making online dating apps, websites, and social media platforms central to how people find romantic partners. While these tools offer new opportunities to meet people beyond one's immediate social circle, they also introduce unique challenges. From carefully curating your online presence to navigating the red flags that often arise in the early stages of dating, understanding how to approach modern dating with a mindful and strategic outlook can make all the difference in finding a meaningful connection.

Online dating has revolutionized the way people seek relationships, offering unprecedented access to potential partners from all walks of life. One of the primary advantages of online dating is the sheer volume of people you can connect with, many of whom you might not encounter in your day-to-day life. Whether you're using dating apps like Tinder, Bumble, or Hinge, or more specific platforms catering to particular interests or demographics, online dating allows you to cast a wide net in your search for love. This expanded access can increase the chances of finding someone compatible, especially if you have a busy lifestyle or live in a smaller community with fewer romantic prospects.

However, online dating also comes with its drawbacks. One of the main challenges is the overwhelming nature of having so many choices. With countless profiles to swipe through, it can be easy to fall into the trap of "shopping" for a partner, treating people as commodities rather than individuals with unique stories and desires. This abundance of choice can also lead to "option paralysis," where users become so fixated on the possibility of finding someone better that they struggle to commit to one person. Additionally, the anonymity and curated nature of online profiles mean that people may present themselves in ways that are not entirely truthful, leading to disappointments or mismatched expectations when meeting in person.

Crafting an authentic online dating profile is key to attracting the right kind of partner and avoiding the pitfalls of misrepresentation. It's tempting to highlight only your best qualities, but creating a profile that reflects your true self will help you attract people who are genuinely compatible with you. Start by choosing photos that not only show you at your best but also offer a glimpse into your personality and lifestyle. Avoid heavily filtered or staged images that don't represent who you are in real life, as this can lead to a disconnect when you eventually meet someone in person. Instead, choose photos that highlight your hobbies, interests, and experiences—whether it's a picture of you hiking, playing an instrument, or enjoying time with friends.

When it comes to writing your bio, authenticity is crucial. Focus on what truly matters to you, whether it's your love for adventure, your passion for your career, or your desire for a meaningful relationship. Be specific in what you're looking for in a partner, but also remain open to discovering someone who might surprise you. Avoid generic phrases like "I love to laugh" or "I'm looking for someone who's down-to-earth," as these don't offer much insight into who you are or what you value. Instead, share a bit about your personal journey, what you're passionate about, and what you hope to experience in a relationship.

Once you've begun connecting with potential partners, it's essential to remain vigilant for red flags in the early stages of dating. Red flags are warning signs that a relationship might not be healthy or fulfilling in the long term. In the context of online dating, these can include behaviors such as inconsistent communication, reluctance to meet in person, or evasiveness about personal details. If someone frequently cancels plans, offers vague explanations for their actions, or makes you feel uneasy about their intentions, it's important to trust your instincts and recognize these as potential red flags.

Another common red flag is when someone moves too fast emotionally. While it's exciting to feel an immediate connection with someone, love-bombing—where a person showers you with excessive attention and affection early on—can be a tactic to establish control and manipulate your emotions. If someone is pushing for a level of commitment or intimacy that feels premature, it's worth taking a step back and evaluating whether their intentions align with your own.

On the flip side, it's equally important to be aware of your own behaviors and ensure that you are presenting yourself honestly and respectfully. Avoid stringing people along if you're unsure of your feelings or keeping conversations superficial just to see how many options you can accumulate. Treat the people you connect with as you would in any real-life interaction—with kindness, honesty, and respect for their time and emotions.

As you navigate these early interactions, establishing clear communication and setting boundaries is vital to laying the groundwork for a healthy relationship. Misunderstandings and mismatched expectations often arise when there's a lack of clarity in communication. Early on, be open about your intentions for the relationship. Whether you're looking for something casual or seeking a long-term commitment, make sure that you and your partner are on the same page to avoid future disappointment.

Setting boundaries is another key aspect of building a strong foundation in a relationship. Boundaries define what you are comfortable with emotionally, physically, and mentally, and they allow both partners to feel safe and respected. In modern dating, boundaries are particularly important as people navigate the complexities of balancing online interactions with in-person meetings. For example, you might establish a boundary around how quickly you want to move from chatting online to meeting in person, or how much personal information you're willing to share in the early stages of getting to know someone.

Being clear about your boundaries also extends to physical and emotional intimacy. Moving too quickly in these areas can sometimes cloud your judgment about the person's true compatibility with you. Taking the time to communicate openly about your comfort level can help both you and your partner feel more secure and respected. It's also a way to test whether your potential partner is attentive and understanding of your needs—an essential quality in any long-term relationship.

Ultimately, the modern dating world can feel overwhelming with its myriad options and fast-paced nature, but approaching it with patience, self-awareness, and a focus on clear communication can help you build a relationship that stands the test of time. While online dating offers convenience and accessibility, it's important to remember that finding the right partner still requires effort, discernment, and a commitment to authenticity. By presenting yourself genuinely, recognizing red flags, and establishing healthy boundaries from the outset, you'll be better positioned to form a meaningful connection that leads to a lasting relationship.

CHAPTER 4: THE ART OF ATTRACTION

Attraction is a complex and multifaceted experience that plays a critical role in how relationships form and evolve. While the initial spark of attraction may ignite a relationship, sustaining it over time requires a deeper connection that transcends physical appearances. Understanding the balance between emotional and physical attraction is key to finding a partner who not only excites you on a surface level but also fulfills you emotionally, intellectually, and spiritually. By learning to navigate the nuances of attraction and differentiating between infatuation and genuine love, you can build a foundation for a relationship that stands the test of time.

Emotional and physical attraction often work hand in hand, but they serve different purposes in the context of a long-term relationship. Physical attraction is usually what draws people together initially. It's the immediate chemistry or allure you feel when you see someone who captivates you. This aspect of attraction can be powerful and intoxicating, often creating a sense of excitement and anticipation in the early stages of dating. However, physical attraction alone is not enough to sustain a relationship over the long term. While it plays an important role in keeping the passion alive, relationships that are built solely on physical attraction tend to fizzle out when deeper emotional bonds are not formed.

On the other hand, emotional attraction is the glue that holds a relationship together in the long run. It's the connection that is built through shared experiences, mutual understanding, and a genuine appreciation for one another's inner qualities. Emotional attraction develops over time as you get to know someone on a deeper level, and it is often what sustains a relationship when the initial excitement of physical attraction begins to fade. When emotional and physical attraction are balanced, they create a relationship that is both passionate and meaningful, providing the foundation for lasting love.

Building meaningful connections requires more than just physical chemistry. It involves cultivating emotional intelligence, empathy, and vulnerability—qualities that allow you to truly understand and connect with your partner on a deep level. Emotional intelligence, or the ability to recognize and manage your own emotions as well as those of others, plays a crucial role in relationship success. It allows you to navigate conflicts, communicate effectively, and respond to your partner's needs in a thoughtful and considerate way.

Empathy is another critical component of building meaningful connections. By putting yourself in your partner's shoes and considering their feelings, you can create a sense of emotional safety and trust that strengthens your bond. When both partners are empathetic toward each other, they are more likely to feel understood, supported, and valued. This mutual understanding fosters a deeper connection and allows for greater emotional intimacy, which is essential for sustaining a long-term relationship.

Vulnerability is perhaps one of the most challenging yet rewarding aspects of building a meaningful connection. In order to create a truly deep bond with someone, you must be willing to let down your guard and share your true self—flaws, fears, and all. Vulnerability is what allows you to connect with your partner on a deeper emotional level, as it invites them to do the same. When both partners are able to be open and honest with one another, it creates a sense of emotional closeness and trust that strengthens the relationship over time. However, being vulnerable also means taking the risk of being hurt, which is why it's important to establish a foundation of trust and mutual respect before opening up fully.

Navigating the line between infatuation and genuine love can be tricky, especially in the early stages of a relationship when emotions are running high. Infatuation often feels like love, but it is typically more focused on the idea of the person rather than who they truly are. It's driven by excitement, passion, and a sense of idealization that can make it easy to overlook red flags or differences in values and goals. Infatuation is often fueled by physical attraction and the thrill of the unknown, which can create a heightened sense of desire and urgency.

While infatuation can be an exhilarating experience, it's important to recognize that it is often fleeting. Over time, as the initial excitement fades and reality sets in, infatuation may give way to disillusionment if the relationship lacks a deeper emotional connection. This is why it's essential to take the time to get to know your partner beyond the surface level and to build a foundation of trust, communication, and mutual respect. Genuine love, on the other hand, is rooted in a deep emotional bond that is built on shared values, goals, and experiences. It is based on a true understanding of and appreciation for your partner's character, rather than just the excitement of being in a new relationship.

In a relationship built on genuine love, both partners are committed to supporting one another's growth and happiness. They are willing to work through challenges together and make compromises, when necessary, because they value the relationship and the emotional connection they have developed. Genuine love is not about trying to change or control the other person; rather, it's about accepting and loving them for who they are, flaws and all. This type of love is grounded in mutual respect, trust, and a shared vision for the future.

One of the key differences between infatuation and genuine love is how each manifest over time. Infatuation tends to be short-lived, often fading once the initial excitement wears off or once the reality of the relationship sets in. Genuine love, however, grows stronger over time as both partners invest in the relationship and build a deeper emotional connection. While the intensity of physical attraction may ebb and flow over the course of the relationship, the emotional bond that comes with genuine love remains a constant source of strength and stability.

To cultivate genuine love, it's important to approach your relationship with patience and intentionality. Take the time to truly get to know your partner and to build a strong foundation of trust and emotional intimacy. This means being open and honest with one another, communicating your needs and desires, and being willing to work through challenges together. By focusing on building a meaningful connection based on shared values and mutual respect, you can create a relationship that is not only passionate but also deeply fulfilling.

In conclusion, the art of attraction involves more than just physical chemistry—it requires emotional intelligence, empathy, vulnerability, and a deep understanding of what makes a relationship last. By balancing emotional and physical attraction, building meaningful connections, and distinguishing between infatuation and genuine love, you can create a relationship that is both passionate and enduring. While the excitement of infatuation may be thrilling, it is the depth of genuine love that will ultimately sustain a relationship and provide the foundation for a lifetime of happiness and fulfillment.

CHAPTER 5: BUILDING A STRONG AND LASTING RELATIONSHIP

In the journey of love, building a strong and lasting relationship requires more than just attraction; it demands a commitment to open communication, mutual respect, and support. These foundational elements are crucial for fostering a bond that withstands the tests of time and adversity. As couples navigate the ups and downs of life together, cultivating effective communication skills becomes paramount in creating an environment of trust and understanding. It is through open, honest conversations that partners can express their feelings, share their thoughts, and address any concerns that may arise.

Effective communication is the cornerstone of a healthy relationship. It allows partners to voice their needs and desires while ensuring that they truly listen to one another. This practice not only fosters a sense of connection but also reinforces the idea that both partners are valued and heard. When couples engage in honest dialogue, they can avoid misunderstandings and build a deeper emotional intimacy that strengthens their bond. It's essential for partners to create a safe space where they can express themselves without fear of judgment, knowing that their thoughts and feelings will be met with compassion and empathy.

However, communication is not always easy, especially during times of conflict. Disagreements are a natural part of any relationship, but how couples handle these conflicts can significantly impact the health of their partnership. Introducing strategies for conflict resolution is vital in ensuring that disagreements are managed respectfully and productively. Rather than resorting to blame or defensiveness, couples can learn to approach conflicts as opportunities for growth and understanding.

One effective strategy for conflict resolution is practicing active listening. This involves not only hearing what the other person is saying but also validating their feelings and showing that their perspective is understood. By paraphrasing their partner's concerns and acknowledging their emotions, couples can diffuse tension and create a collaborative environment for problem-solving. Additionally, it is essential to focus on the issue at hand rather than bringing up past grievances or engaging in personal attacks. By addressing the specific conflict and working together to find a solution, partners can strengthen their relationship and demonstrate their commitment to one another.

Another important aspect of maintaining a healthy relationship is mutual respect and support. Partners should recognize that they are each individual with their own goals, dreams, and aspirations. By actively supporting one another's personal growth, couples can create a nurturing environment that fosters both individual and collective success. This support can take many forms, such as encouraging each other to pursue hobbies, advance in their careers, or take on new challenges. Celebrating each other's achievements, no matter how small, reinforces the bond between partners and instills a sense of teamwork within the relationship.

In addition to mutual respect and support, maintaining intimacy and connection is crucial for the longevity of a relationship. As time passes, couples may find that the initial excitement of their romance begins to fade. To counter this, it is important to prioritize both emotional and physical intimacy. Emotionally, partners can stay connected by engaging in meaningful conversations, sharing experiences, and expressing affection regularly. This can involve simple gestures, such as holding hands, cuddling, or verbal affirmations of love and appreciation.

Physical intimacy also plays a significant role in maintaining closeness. It's important for couples to nurture their sexual connection, as this aspect of the relationship can significantly impact overall satisfaction. Setting aside time for intimacy, exploring new experiences together, and openly discussing desires and boundaries can help keep the spark alive. Moreover, emotional intimacy is often enhanced through physical connection, as acts of affection can deepen the emotional bond between partners.

As relationships evolve, it is natural for couples to experience changes in their emotional and physical connections. However, by actively nurturing these aspects, partners can ensure that their bond remains strong, even in the face of challenges. This requires intentionality and commitment from both individuals to prioritize their relationship amidst the demands of daily life.

Ultimately, building a strong and lasting relationship involves a combination of effective communication, conflict resolution, mutual respect, and intimacy. By fostering an environment of openness and understanding, couples can navigate challenges together and strengthen their emotional connection. Supporting one another's growth and maintaining closeness, both emotionally and physically, creates a resilient partnership that can thrive through life's ups and downs. With dedication and effort, couples can cultivate a relationship that not only endures but flourishes, bringing lasting joy and fulfillment to both partners.

CHAPTER 6: CHOOSING THE RIGHT PARTNER: SIGNS OF A HEALTHY RELATIONSHIP

In the quest for love, choosing the right partner stands as a critical milestone that can profoundly shape the trajectory of your life. Understanding the signs of a healthy relationship is essential in ensuring that your journey is not just fulfilling but also sustainable. One of the key indicators of a suitable partner is emotional maturity. This quality encompasses a partner's ability to handle their emotions, navigate challenges, and take on responsibilities with a sense of composure and accountability. An emotionally mature partner approaches conflicts with a calm demeanor, engages in constructive discussions, and expresses their feelings in a healthy manner, paving the way for a harmonious relationship.

Recognizing emotional maturity involves observing how your partner reacts to stressful situations. Do they engage in open dialogue when disagreements arise, or do they resort to defensiveness and avoidance? A partner who can acknowledge their feelings, communicate effectively, and work toward resolutions demonstrates a level of maturity that is vital for a successful partnership. This emotional stability fosters a safe environment for both individuals to express their vulnerabilities, ultimately strengthening their bond.

In addition to emotional maturity, shared future visions play a crucial role in determining whether a relationship is worth pursuing. Ensuring that both partners have compatible visions of the future, including family aspirations, career goals, and personal growth, can help build a solid foundation for a lasting partnership. Open discussions about where each partner sees themselves in the coming years are essential. Couples should explore topics such as marriage, children, career ambitions, and lifestyle preferences. When both partners align their goals, it creates a sense of unity and purpose, allowing them to work together toward a common future.

Conversely, mismatched future visions can lead to significant challenges and heartache. If one partner envisions a large family while the other prefers a life of independence, the resulting tensions can jeopardize the relationship. It is vital to have these conversations early on, as they reveal not only compatibility but also the willingness of each partner to support the other's dreams. Healthy relationships are characterized by partners who uplift and inspire each other to pursue their aspirations, even if those aspirations evolve over time.

Trust and commitment serve as the bedrock of a healthy relationship. The importance of mutual trust cannot be overstated; it forms the basis for emotional safety and security between partners. Trust is cultivated through consistent actions, open communication, and a willingness to be vulnerable. When both individuals feel confident in each other's intentions and reliability, they are more likely to invest deeply in the relationship.

Commitment goes hand in hand with trust, as it reflects the dedication of both partners to making the relationship work. This commitment requires a mutual understanding that challenges may arise but that both individuals are willing to face them together. It's about being present for one another, especially during difficult times, and prioritizing the relationship above external distractions. Commitment manifests through actions—being there for your partner, supporting their goals, and standing by them during trials— all of which reinforce the strength of the bond.

Growing together, not apart, is another vital aspect of choosing the right partner. Life is a journey of continuous change, and healthy relationships thrive on the growth of both individuals, both independently and as a couple. Partners should encourage each other to pursue personal interests and goals while also engaging in shared experiences that deepen their connection. This balance ensures that both individuals feel fulfilled in their personal lives, which, in turn, positively impacts the relationship.

It's important to recognize that growth is not always linear; there will be periods of uncertainty and change. However, couples who prioritize communication and mutual support during these transitions are better equipped to navigate life's challenges together. This might mean revisiting shared goals or exploring new paths as a team. Regular check-ins about personal aspirations and emotional well-being can help partners stay aligned and connected as they evolve together.

Ultimately, choosing the right partner involves recognizing signs of a healthy relationship, such as emotional maturity, shared future visions, trust, commitment, and the ability to grow together. By cultivating these elements, individuals can create a strong foundation for love that not only endures but thrives through life's many changes. In this pursuit, the journey of love becomes an enriching experience that transforms both partners, leading to a fulfilling and lasting relationship that enhances their lives together.

CHAPTER 7: AVOIDING COMMON RELATIONSHIP PITFALLS

In the journey of love, one of the most critical aspects is the ability to avoid common relationship pitfalls that can hinder happiness and personal growth. The danger of settling for a partner out of fear or pressure can lead to a life of dissatisfaction and unfulfilled potential. Many individuals find themselves in relationships that do not serve their best interests simply because they are afraid of being alone or feel societal pressure to conform to a certain timeline. This settling can manifest in various ways, from tolerating disrespectful behavior to ignoring fundamental incompatibilities. It is essential to recognize that true fulfillment comes from being with someone who complements your life rather than simply filling a void.

Holding out for the right partner means prioritizing your emotional well-being and understanding that a healthy relationship is built on mutual respect, shared values, and genuine connection. The fear of loneliness or the pressure to be in a relationship can cloud judgment, causing individuals to overlook crucial red flags. It's vital to cultivate patience and self-awareness, allowing yourself the time to find a partner who aligns with your aspirations and values. The process may be challenging, but the rewards of waiting for someone who truly resonates with you are immeasurable.

Recognizing toxic relationships is another crucial aspect of maintaining a healthy romantic life. Toxic behavior can manifest in numerous ways, including manipulation, control, and emotional abuse. Identifying these signs early on can prevent significant emotional harm and pave the way for healthier connections. Manipulation often presents itself as guilt-tripping or emotional blackmail, where one partner attempts to control the other's actions through emotional coercion. Control can take various forms, from monitoring your social interactions to dictating your choices. Emotional abuse, on the other hand, may involve belittling, gaslighting, or undermining your self-worth.

Understanding these behaviors is key to establishing boundaries and recognizing when it's time to exit a relationship. If you find yourself in a toxic situation, it's essential to trust your instincts and seek support from trusted friends or professionals. Exiting such relationships can be challenging, but prioritizing your mental and emotional health must take precedence. Remember, it's better to be single than to stay in a relationship that diminishes your self-worth and happiness.

While the importance of independence in a relationship is often overlooked, it plays a vital role in maintaining a healthy partnership. When individuals lose themselves in a relationship, neglecting personal interests, friendships, and passions, it can lead to resentment and a lack of fulfillment. Healthy partnerships thrive when both individuals maintain their identities and nurture their personal growth. Engaging in individual activities not only enriches your life but also brings fresh energy into the relationship.

Maintaining personal independence involves setting aside time for hobbies, interests, and friendships outside the relationship. This independence fosters self-growth and allows partners to bring unique experiences and perspectives into the relationship. It encourages both individuals to grow together while also supporting each other's individual journeys. When both partners are invested in their personal development, it creates a dynamic and enriching relationship that withstands the test of time.

Breaking the cycle of bad relationship patterns is crucial for personal growth and healthier future connections. Many individuals unconsciously repeat unhealthy dynamics from past relationships, often due to unresolved emotional wounds or ingrained beliefs about love and partnership. Recognizing these patterns requires introspection and honesty with oneself. Take the time to reflect on past relationships—what went wrong, what behaviors contributed to the breakdown, and how those experiences shaped your views on love.

Once you've identified these patterns, it's essential to consciously work toward breaking them. This might involve seeking therapy or counseling to address underlying issues and develop healthier coping mechanisms. Additionally, being mindful in your current relationship and paying attention to triggers can help prevent the repetition of past mistakes. Communication is key; openly discussing your experiences and desires with your partner can foster a deeper understanding and prevent misunderstandings.

As you navigate the complexities of relationships, remember that avoiding common pitfalls requires a commitment to self-awareness, patience, and the willingness to prioritize your well-being. Recognize the danger of settling, learn to identify toxic behaviors, maintain your independence, and consciously break unhealthy patterns. By doing so, you lay a strong foundation for a fulfilling, loving partnership that supports both your individual growth and your shared journey together. Embrace the process, and trust that the love you've been waiting for is worth the effort and commitment to find it.

CHAPTER 8: PREPARING FOR A LASTING FUTURE

In the quest for lasting love, preparation is a crucial component that many overlook, often leading to unexpected challenges down the road. Recognizing the role of patience and timing in love can profoundly impact the quality and longevity of a relationship. Finding the right partner is often less about aggressive pursuit and more about waiting for the right circumstances to align. Love cannot be rushed; it flourishes when nurtured over time. Timing plays an essential role, not just in meeting someone but in being emotionally and mentally ready to embrace a new relationship. Life experiences, personal growth, and readiness to commit must all coincide for a relationship to thrive.

Sometimes, patience is the most challenging part of the process, especially in a fast-paced society that often glorifies immediate gratification. It's essential to cultivate a mindset that values waiting for someone who genuinely fits your life and goals. Instead of feeling pressure to settle down, use this time to focus on your personal development and self-discovery. This period of introspection allows you to understand what you truly want in a partner and ensures that when the right person arrives, you are equipped to recognize and appreciate them fully.

However, commitment in a relationship extends beyond romance. As partners choose to build a life together, addressing the practical aspects of their shared future becomes imperative. This includes navigating the complexities of finances, career decisions, and family planning. Financial discussions may be uncomfortable, yet they are essential for a healthy partnership. Understanding each other's financial habits, goals, and expectations can prevent conflicts later on. Couples should work together to create a budget that accommodates both partners' needs while also setting aside funds for shared experiences and future investments.

Career decisions are equally important, as they can significantly affect a couple's dynamic. Whether one partner has aspirations that require relocation, long hours, or additional education, discussing how these decisions impact the relationship is vital. Ensuring that both partners feel supported in their professional endeavors fosters mutual respect and strengthens the partnership. Open dialogue about career ambitions helps to avoid feelings of resentment and allows each person to thrive in their respective paths.

Family planning is another significant aspect of preparing for a lasting future. As relationships deepen, discussing the desire for children, parenting styles, and family values becomes increasingly necessary. This conversation can be daunting, but aligning on family goals early on lays the groundwork for a solid partnership. It's important to consider each partner's upbringing, cultural background, and personal beliefs about family life. Being transparent about these aspects can lead to deeper understanding and connection.

Continual growth as a couple is a vital element in maintaining a healthy, thriving relationship. Relationships are dynamic and evolve over time; therefore, partners must prioritize both personal and relational growth. Encouraging one another to pursue individual interests, hobbies, and personal development not only enriches each partner's life but also brings fresh energy into the relationship. Taking the time to reflect on your experiences, goals, and aspirations helps ensure that both individuals continue to grow together while also nurturing their own identities.

Engaging in activities that foster growth—such as attending workshops, reading books together, or participating in counseling—can provide valuable insights and tools for relationship enhancement. Being proactive in seeking growth opportunities reinforces a commitment to the relationship and demonstrates a willingness to invest time and effort into nurturing the bond.

Planning for the future as a couple involves balancing individual ambitions with shared goals. This process requires open communication about aspirations, dreams, and priorities. Creating a shared vision for the future helps both partners stay aligned and focused on their mutual objectives. Whether it involves travel, financial milestones, or personal achievements, outlining these goals together fosters a sense of unity and purpose.

Setting short-term and long-term goals as a couple can create a roadmap for your relationship. Regular check-ins to discuss progress and reassess priorities can help partners stay on track. Flexibility is also key; as life changes, so too might your plans and ambitions. Embracing change together strengthens the partnership and allows both individuals to feel heard and valued.

As you prepare for a lasting future, remember that love is not just a feeling but a commitment to growth, understanding, and shared aspirations. By recognizing the importance of patience and timing, addressing practical matters of life together, fostering continual growth, and planning collectively for the future, you lay the groundwork for a deep, meaningful partnership. Love flourishes when nurtured with intention and effort, creating a bond that stands the test of time. Embrace the journey, and trust that the love you've been waiting for will not only arrive but will also thrive when nurtured with care and commitment.

CONCLUSION

In the intricate tapestry of love and relationships, the journey to finding lasting love is often filled with twists and turns, challenges and revelations. Embracing this process is essential, as it teaches us invaluable lessons about ourselves and what we seek in a partner. Recognizing that finding the right partner is not merely a destination but a journey allows us to appreciate each step along the way. Each experience, whether joyful or painful, shapes our understanding of love and prepares us for the connection we truly desire.

As we navigate this journey, trusting ourselves becomes a cornerstone of success. The self-awareness gained through understanding our values, needs, and emotional triggers equips us with the tools necessary to attract the right partner. Healing past wounds is equally crucial; it frees us from the burdens of previous relationships and enables us to enter new connections with a clean slate. By setting clear intentions for what we want in a partner and relationship, we open ourselves to possibilities that align with our authentic selves. Trusting in our ability to discern who complements us allows for healthier connections built on mutual respect and understanding.

Moving forward with confidence is a powerful mindset to cultivate as we seek lasting love. Confidence does not stem from perfection or the absence of fear; instead, it arises from embracing our journey, acknowledging our worth, and believing that we deserve a fulfilling relationship. Each step we take—whether it involves putting ourselves out there in the dating world, navigating potential pitfalls, or having difficult conversations—becomes an opportunity to reinforce our self-assuredness.

In a society often marked by instant gratification and fleeting connections, committing to the pursuit of meaningful love requires patience and resilience. Trusting the timing of our journey allows us to recognize that true love is worth waiting for, and each experience is a stepping stone toward that goal. The process may not always be straightforward, but by staying true to ourselves, remaining open to growth, and nurturing our relationships, we are actively participating in the creation of a loving partnership.

Ultimately, finding lasting love is about aligning our lives with those who resonate with our core values and aspirations. It is a process that calls for introspection, courage, and a willingness to embrace vulnerability. As we engage with our emotions and desires, we pave the way for connections that are not only fulfilling but also transformative. By trusting ourselves and the journey we undertake, we cultivate an unwavering belief that the love we seek is not just a dream but a reality waiting to unfold.

In conclusion, the journey to finding lasting love is rich with opportunities for growth, self-discovery, and connection. By embracing the process, trusting ourselves, and moving forward with confidence, we open the door to the love we've been waiting for—a love that is deep, meaningful, and resilient. Each moment spent on this journey brings us closer to the partner who will walk beside us, sharing in life's joys and challenges, and ultimately, creating a bond that endures the test of time.